Perspectives
Playing Competitive Sports
Is Competition Good For Children?

Series Consultant: Linda Hoyt

Flying Start to Literacy®

Contents

Are competitive sports good for children?

Some people love playing competitive sports. Others definitely don't. The advantages and disadvantages of children participating in competitive sports has long been debated.

What about you? Would you rather be active without the pressure of winning or losing? Have you ever fell too much pressure when competing?

How do you cope with competitive pressure? Does it help you? Or does it make you too anxious to play well?

Sporting greats

Some superstars love what they do, while others don't. Here, three successful sportspeople share their thoughts on playing sport.

What do these quotes tell you about these sporting greats?

"Somewhere behind the athlete you've become and the hours of practice and the coaches who have pushed you, is a little girl who fell in love with a game and never looked back ... play for her."

Mia Hamm, award-winning professional soccer player, 1987–2004

"I'm seven years old, talking to myself, because I'm scared, and because I'm the only person who listens to me. Under my breath I whisper: Just quit Andre, just give up . . . But I can't. Not only would my father chase me around the house with my racket, but something in my gut, some deep unseen muscle, won't let me. I hate tennis, hate it with all my heart, and still I keep playing, keep hitting all morning, and all afternoon, because I have no choice."

Andre Agassi, former world No. 1 tennis player, from his autobiography Open, *2009*

"Coming into my first Olympics I didn't think I was going to be getting a gold medal individually. My goal was just to get more experience, swim as fast as I can. And after prelims and semi-finals and seeing where I was sitting, when I came in tonight I was like, 'I want to get on that medal stand.' Just surpassing that goal and getting an American record on top of a gold medal is super exciting for me."

Simone Manuel, gold medal winner,
100 metre freestyle, Olympics 2016,
Rio de Janeiro, Brazil

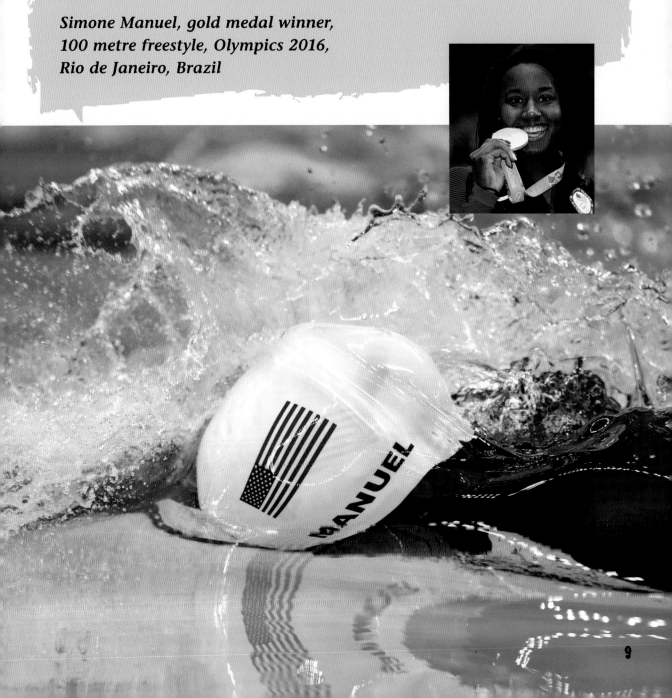

Playing to win or just playing?

Many people assume that competitive sports have positive effects as long as we approach them with the right attitude. But Alfie Kohn, author of *No Contest: The Case Against Competition*, asks us to consider whether there's something wrong with activities where having fun requires people to defeat one another.

Does this article raise any questions about competition that you haven't considered before?

It's kind of weird, when you think about it: The way we're supposed to have fun is for a bunch of people to try to defeat another bunch of people. The games we're familiar with are set up so everyone can't achieve their goal. One group can succeed only by making the other group fail.

Half the people may cheer at the end, but their satisfaction doesn't last very long. And the results also tend to include gloating (by the winners), disappointment (by the losers), nasty behaviour and cheating. No matter how many times those things happen, individual players are blamed as if it's all their fault.

It took me a while to figure out that the problem really lies not with the competitors, but with the whole idea of competition – activities that sort us into winners and losers. When people claim that competition is fine as long as it's done right, they never support that statement with evidence. That's because there isn't any.

What scientific evidence actually shows is that when people compete, they come to believe they're valuable only when they keep winning. Unfortunately, nobody wins all the time. Research also shows that competition makes people less trusting, less honest in their communication, less likely to help those in need and less likely to imagine how things look from other people's perspectives.

04

Again, all these negative effects are experienced by winners as well as losers. And they don't prove that people have the wrong attitude about competition. These problems are predictable results of competition itself.

That's not a popular conclusion because we're taught not only to compete but also to believe in competition – to assume it's "just the way life is" and that it motivates people to do their best. But both of these beliefs are false. Some people – in fact, some whole cultures – aren't competitive at all. If we compete, it's because we're raised that way, not because we're born that way.

And, surprisingly, competition doesn't usually help us do our best. There are basically three ways of doing something: apart from others (independently), with others (cooperatively) or against others (competitively). Lots of studies have shown that struggling against others is the least effective.

That's true for three reasons. First, competition makes many people anxious, and anxiety gets in the way of doing well.

Second, when you do something (like swimming or painting) in order to get a trophy or a prize, you start to lose interest in the swimming or painting itself. Now the point is just to get the prize. And when we don't enjoy what we're doing, we usually don't do it well.

Third, what really helps people to succeed is cooperation – learning from and supporting each other. But competitive sports limit cooperation to teams, and, worse, the point is to defeat other teams. The most successful (and enjoyable) activities are those where everyone can work, or learn, or play together – not activities where it's me against you, or us against them.

When kids say they like sports, it may be because they don't know there are other ways to have fun! One study found that when young children were introduced to purely cooperative games as well as the usual competitive games (football, basketball, baseball), most of them liked the cooperative games much better.

Lots of people steer us to ask the little questions: Are we competing the right amount? In the right way? But it takes some courage to step back and ask the big question: Should we be competing at all?

A coach's view

In this interview, ex-NBA player for the New Jersey Nets and basketball coach, Joe Hooks, talks about his experience playing competitive sport.

What does taking part in competitive sports mean to you?

Coach Joe Hooks

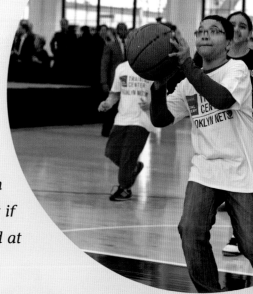

Is competition good for kids?

It depends on the environment in which you come from. For me it was a way out. I grew up on a farm and my dad was up at four o'clock every morning. It was tough work. What I learnt from my dad was that if I wanted a different life, I had to work hard at being good at what I chose to do.

How did you come to basketball?

My uncles played basketball and I spent lots of time with them. On weekends, they would come and get me and we would play basketball, then we would watch the games. In Grade 8, I missed out on making the school team. If you don't make the school team, there are no other options. You're either in or out. I didn't give up, I kept playing – before school, lunchtime, after school – I was always playing even though I didn't make the team. The next year, I made the team.

What life skills does playing competitive sports give kids?

For me, it was a way to get on with other people. I was artistic and was happy in my own company. I loved to draw pen and ink drawings. I had an art exhibition as a seven-year-old. I spent lots of time on my own. Playing basketball gave me a way to engage with other people. What I also learnt was to give it your best. Trying your hardest is more important than winning all the time. We have to teach kids that you can't win all the time, but that you can learn from your losses you look at your game and make adjustments to what you are doing to give yourself a better chance. Losing is about making adjustments and continuing to pursue your goal.

Fun and games

Kelsie Ingham writes that games and sports have been an essential part of the lives of the Native American people for centuries.

Can you think of reasons why some games and sports were played with everyone – young and old – on the teams? How does this compare with the sports and games we play today?

Just as they are for today's children, games and sports were an important part of the lives of children growing up before 1492, in the pre-Columbian era in North America. Native American kids – and adults, too – enjoyed a variety of games and sports. But they weren't just pastimes: they also taught life lessons and skills. Games and sports were for everyone: men, women, children and the elderly. Some games were played by one person, and others were team sports that could include an entire village.

Through play, children learnt valuable skills. Many children's games mimicked adult behaviour, such as hunting and stalking. Practising silent footsteps and quiet breathing while sneaking up on someone was fun, and it trained children to be good hunters. (Haven't you had fun sneaking up on a friend or parent?) Running games and races were popular. Running was useful for hunting and gathering food and for delivering messages in a hurry. Races were run over short and long distances – up to 40 kilometres – and often involved obstacles such as trees or rivers. For some races, children had to spin around, then run while dizzy! These runners improved their balance as well as their speed and endurance.

Groups of children played many different sports. Team sports included everyone, regardless of their skill level. Teams played to win, but fair play and good teamwork were just as important as winning. Many games had judges, but individual players were expected to play fairly. Poor sports and cheaters were punished.

Ball games were popular with some groups, using balls made out of carved bone or wood. Sometimes small pieces of animal skins were stitched together and stuffed to make a ball. Most ball games involved hitting or kicking the ball. While fair play and good teamwork were important, games were rough and rules were few. Women and girls often played separately from men and boys.

Six hundred years ago, kids played tug-of-war and guessing games.
They traded with each other and competed for the best prizes. Boys
and girls played together and separately, having fun and learning
skills they would use when they grew up. Many games we play today
came from Native American sports. Rough-and-tumble competition,
yes. But teamwork and cooperation are an equally important part of
the legacy of these first American games.

The day I wasn't selected

You have been friends forever. You like the same things. You play the same sports. You're on the same team. But then one day it all changes. You have to compete to be on the same team as your friends.

Here, 14-year-old Callum Gillespie recalls the day when playing on the same team as his friends was no longer a given.

How would you feel in the same situation?

Back about six years ago, I was really into soccer. My friends and I lived for soccer. Whenever we could, we would go out and kick a soccer ball at the park or somewhere.

The first club that we played for was called Elwood City. It was really relaxed with an extremely diverse range of skills. My friends and I played for this club for two years and for the most part we liked it.

But by the end of the second year we were looking for a team with a higher skill level. My friends and I wanted to play for a competitive club that had organised practices. The team we wanted to join was an elite team and you were required to try out if you wanted to play.

I can remember that for the entire week before the tryouts took place, I was genuinely shaking. I was so nervous, I didn't perform as well as I could at the tryouts.

About a week later, I distinctly remember my mum waking me up and being super nice. Then she sat me down and told me the bad news – I didn't get in the team and all my friends did. I was so sad and angry. I remember my head feeling like it was on fire. I cried and I cried and I cried until I had no tears left.

Based on my experiences, I do not believe that such young kids should be subjected to so much grief over a recreational activity. But some of my greatest memories are of playing soccer and I have also made some lifelong friends.

In conclusion, I do believe that young kids should be allowed the privilege to play competitive sports. I just don't think there should be so much pressure on them to make the team because at the end of the day, sport is for fun.

What is your opinion?: How to write a persuasive argument

1. State your opinion

Think about the issues related to your topic. What is your opinion?

2. Research

Research the information you need to support your opinion.

Related PERSPECTIVES book   Internet   Other sources

3. Make a plan

Introduction

How will you "hook" the reader?

State your opinion.

List reasons to support your opinion.

What persuasive devices will you use?

| **Reason 1** | **Reason 2** | **Reason 3** |
| Support your reason with evidence and details. | Support your reason with evidence and details. | Support your reason with evidence and details. |

Conclusion

Restate your opinion. Leave your reader with a strong message.

4. Publish

Publish your persuasive argument.

Use visuals to reinforce your opinion.